Best Mas

Root Management
Second Edition

Laurence R. Costello
Gary Watson
E. Thomas Smiley
Richard Hauer

International Society of
Arboriculture

ISBN: 978-1-943378-29-6

Copyright © 2017, 2023 by International Society of Arboriculture

All rights reserved.

Printed in the United States of America.

Except as permitted under the United States Copyright Act of 1976, no part of this publication may be reproduced or distributed in any form or by any means or stored in a database or retrieval system without the prior written permission of the International Society of Arboriculture (ISA).

Standards and regulations such as ANSI, OSHA, ISO, and others regionally and internationally may have specific requirements for use of "shall," "should," and "must." For the sake of readability and to account for differences between standards, this publication does not necessarily parallel the requirements of such standards or regulations in the use of these terms

Cover Design: Veridian Design Group
Cover Photo: E. Thomas Smiley
Page Design and Composition: Veridian Design Group
Illustrations: Bryan Kotwica
Printed by Gasch Printing, Odenton, MD

International Society of Arboriculture
270 Peachtree St. NW, Suite 1900
Atlanta, GA 30303
United States of America

Gray's Inn House
127 Clerkenwell Road
London EC1R 5DB
United Kingdom

10 9 8 7 6 5 4 3 2
1023-CA-1000

Contents

Acknowledgments

The *Root Management* Best Management Practices (Second Edition) Review Committee:

Scott Baker, Tree Solutions, Seattle, WA

Jon Banks, Bartlett Tree Experts, Reading, Berkshire, United Kingdom

Nina Bassuk, Urban Horticulture Institute, Cornell University, Ithaca, NY

Maryellen Bell, Bartlett Tree Experts, Austin, TX

Andrew Benson, The Tree Consultancy Company, Auckland, New Zealand

Patrick Brewer, Bartlett Tree Experts, Austin, TX

Els Couenberg, Natura Ingenium, Manchester, United Kingdom

Susan D. Day, University of British Columbia, Vancouver, Canada

Andreas Detter, Brudi & Partner TreeConsult and SAG Baumstatik e.V., Gauting, Germany

Scott Diffenderfer, Town of Vienna, VA

Andrew Driscoll, Montgomery Parks, Gaithersburg, MD

Alessio Fini, Department of Agricultural and Environmental Sciences – Production, Landscape, Agroenergy, University of Milan, Italy

Jason Grabosky, Rutgers University, New Brunswick, NJ

Jason C. Hasaka, Bartlett Consulting, Bartlett Tree Experts, Bristol, United Kingdom

Donald Hodel, University of California Cooperative Extension, Los Angeles, CA

Mark J. Hoenigman, Busy Bee Services, Novelty, OH

Kent E. Holm, Douglas County Environmental Services, Omaha, NE

Ken James, K. James and Associates, Melbourne, Australia

Jamie Lim, Central Park Conservancy, New York, NY

Gordon Mann, California Tree and Landscape Consulting, Auburn, CA

Greg Moore, University of Melbourne, Melbourne, Australia

Glynn Percival, Bartlett Tree Experts, Reading, Berkshire, United Kingdom

Craig Pinkalla, Minneapolis Park & Recreation Board, Minneapolis, MN

Lindsey Purcell, Indiana Arborist Association, Franklin, IN

Gary Raffel, Bartlett Tree Experts, Rochester, NY

Thomas Barfoed Randrup, Swedish University of Agricultural Sciences, Alnarp, Sweden

Chad M. Rigsby, Bartlett Tree Research Laboratories, Lisle, IL

Christopher Riley, Bartlett Tree Research Laboratories, Washington, DC

Jessica Sanders, Sacramento Tree Foundation, Sacramento, CA

Grant L. Thompson, Genus Landscape Architects, Des Moines, IA

Rick Till, Honl Tree Care, Portland, OR

James Urban, Fellow of the American Society of Landscape Architects, Annapolis, MD

Nicolaas Verloop, TFI Vital Green, Harmelen, The Netherlands

Ellen Vincent, Clemson University, Clemson, SC

Walter Warriner, Los Angeles, CA

Tyler Wilcox, New York City Department of Parks and Recreation, New York, NY

Mark Williams, City Urban Forester, Fort Lauderdale, FL

Purpose

The International Society of Arboriculture (ISA) has developed a series of Best Management Practices (BMPs) for the purpose of interpreting tree care standards and providing guidelines of best practice for arborists, tree workers, and the people who employ their services.

This BMP describes recommended practices for inspecting, pruning, and directing the roots of trees in the built environment. It serves as the companion publication for the *American National Standard for Tree Care Operations — Tree, Shrub, and Other Woody Plant Management — Standard Practices (Root Management)* (ANSI A300, Part 8), but it is also intended to support standards from other countries. The closely related ANSI A300 Standard Part 5, *Management of Trees and Shrubs During Site Planning, Site Development, and Construction,* and its associated BMP *(Managing Trees During Site Development and Construction)* go more deeply into the protection of trees and their root systems during construction. In addition, ANSI A300 Part 2, *Soil Management*, and its two companion BMPs *(Soil Management for Urban Trees* and *Tree and Shrub Fertilization)* provide additional information on managing soil and nutrients.

Because trees and other plants are unique living organisms, not all practices will be relevant to every situation. A qualified arborist should therefore write or review contracts, specifications, and reports using applicable standards and this BMP. Departures from the standards should be made with careful consideration of the objectives and with supporting rationale.

1. Introduction

Roots are an essential component of all trees. They anchor and support trees, absorb water and minerals, store carbohydrates, and produce hormones that regulate growth. In the built environment, tree health and stability can be affected by human activities that disturb the soil, restrict root development, or damage roots.

Infrastructure such as building foundations, streets, sidewalks, and underground structures or utilities can limit the volume of soil available for root development. Traffic on the soil surface and construction or repair of that infrastructure can result in soil disturbance and root damage. Disturbed soil may be compacted so that it limits water infiltration or drainage, restricts root growth, or lacks nutrient availability. Without planning for tree growth there may be inadequate distances between trees and infrastructure. This can result in damage to infrastructure, eventual tree removal, or root damage done to protect the infrastructure. If root damage is severe, trees may become unstable. Decay associated with the root damage may lead to progressive loss of health or stability, and tree death or tree failure may follow.

To maximize tree health and stability as well as minimize infrastructure conflicts, there are a number of root management practices that can be implemented. As with all arboricultural treatments, the objective(s) of the treatment should be clearly defined so the arborist and client understand the treatment, intended outcomes, and limitations.

This BMP addresses three aspects of root management: root inspection, **root pruning**, and minimizing conflicts with infrastructure. The process of root management is illustrated in Figure 1, and details for preparing a root management contract are discussed in Appendix 1. Practices and factors (tree and site) that may contribute to root system failure are addressed in Appendix 2.

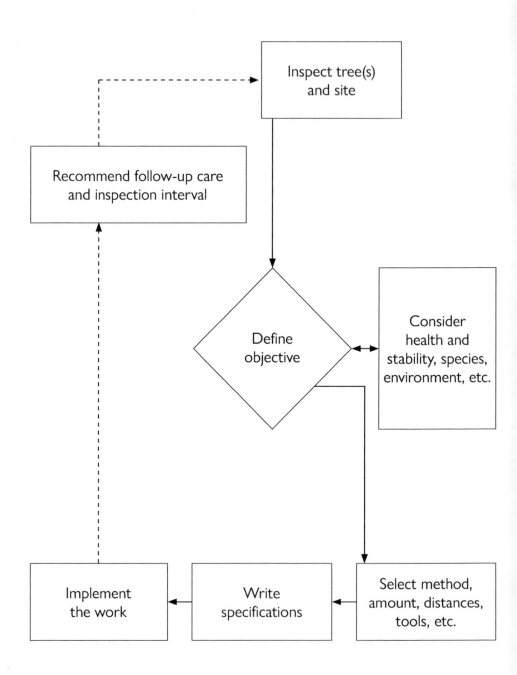

Figure 1. The process of root management, as illustrated in the ANSI A300 Part 8 Standard.

2. Root Systems

Roots: Types, Systems, and Distribution

To manage roots effectively, knowledge of root types, systems, and root distribution is important. This knowledge will serve as a basis for making informed decisions for defining and applying root management practices.

Types of Roots

Trees have five basic types of roots: tap roots, lateral roots, oblique roots, sinker roots, and fine roots (Figure 2). The number and size of each root type varies substantially with tree species, age, and soil conditions.

Tap Root

The first root to emerge from the seed is the radical. It forms the primary root axis from which most other roots originate. As the seedling grows, the radical develops into a **tap root**. This is the dominant downward-growing root. Its diameter is largest immediately beneath the stem and soil surface, and it tapers with depth. A rapidly growing tap root provides access to water

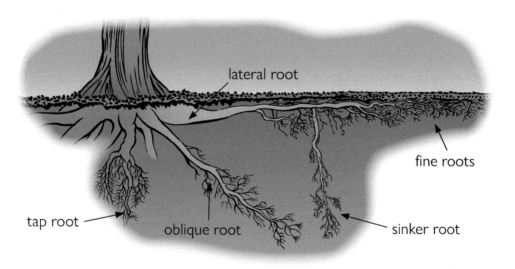

Figure 2. Five basic types of tree roots: tap roots, lateral roots, oblique roots, sinker roots, and fine roots. The number and size of each root type vary substantially with species, age, and soil conditions.

and minerals deeper in the soil, which is important for seedling survival. Some tree species have larger tap roots than others, but tap root growth eventually slows and, in many cases, stops due to root severance, limiting soil conditions, or tree genetics.

Trees transplanted into the landscape usually lack a tap root. In nursery trees, tap root development is often disrupted when trees are undercut for transplanting or trees are grown in containers.

Lateral Roots

Lateral roots arise from the seedling tap root or the base of the trunk and are located near the soil surface. They grow deeper if the surface soil conditions are unfavorable. Lateral root diameter decreases over relatively short distances from the trunk (called the zone of rapid taper), transitioning to long, horizontal, untapered, ropelike roots. Similar to other root types, lateral roots develop side branches over their entire length, which divide repeatedly and terminate as fine roots. Lateral roots and fine roots play a major role in anchorage as well as the absorption and transportation of water and minerals.

As both the trunk and lateral roots enlarge and growth increases as a response to stem movement, the **root flare** (also called the flare, **trunk flare**, or root collar) develops. The lateral roots and the root flare are the principal parts of the root system that damage sidewalks and street curbs.

Lateral roots with buttressing are often called **buttress roots**. Buttressing is the development of wood tissue on the upper part of the union between the lateral root and trunk. Buttresses develop in response to dynamic wind loading and species-specific genetic traits. They serve to disperse mechanical stress at the base of the tree and increase stability.

Oblique Roots

Oblique roots develop from the tap root and/or shallow lateral roots near the base of the trunk. They angle downward between the vertical orientation of the tap root and horizontal orientation of the lateral roots. Generally, oblique roots branch several times, are smaller in diameter than the tap root, and play an important role in anchorage as well as the uptake and transportation of water and minerals.

Sinker Roots

Sinker roots originate along lateral roots and generally occur within the **drip line**. They grow vertically downward, penetrating as much as several feet (about 1 m), but they vary in both length and branching characteristics depending on species and soil conditions. Sinker roots play a key role in accessing water and minerals deeper in the soil profile at times when surface soils become depleted. Sinker roots also serve a role in anchoring the tree.

Fine Roots

Fine roots are nonwoody roots less than 2 mm (0.08 in) in diameter. They initiate from all types of woody roots. Fine roots are most common near the soil surface where soil density, water, and nutrient levels are favorable for growth. They grow in all directions and branch many times. With many branches and close association with soil particles, fine roots aid in anchoring the tree to the soil. Fine roots are relatively short lived and are continually replaced. When soil conditions, such as temperature and moisture, are harsh for even short periods, the rate of root loss can exceed the rate of replacement. When conditions improve, replacement exceeds loss. This fine-root turnover is an important contributor to soil organic matter, possibly exceeding the contribution of fallen and decaying leaves and branches.

Fine roots can be colonized by symbiotic fungi called **mycorrhizae**. By growing extensively throughout the soil, these fungi increase water and mineral uptake and provide a level of protection against certain fungal pathogens. Mycorrhizae utilize carbohydrates that are lost from tree roots and may also link root systems from different trees, allowing the exchange of carbohydrates and hormones. Fine roots and mycorrhizae are the principal points of entry for water and nutrients from the soil.

Adventitious Roots

Adventitious roots are roots that arise from other roots, branches, or stems and originate from lateral meristems. Adventitious roots are true roots, but their origin is different from the five basic root types in that they do not arise from the primary root axis. In some species, they can grow from branches or trunks that are in contact with moist soil or organic matter or from buried trunks.

Adventitious roots absorb water and minerals and may provide structural support when they are large enough. They play an important role when lateral, oblique, sinker, and fine roots are lost due to injury, pruning, or changes in the soil environment. Trees with a genetic capacity for developing adventitious roots can be more resilient to root damage. However, on root-damaged trees, adventitious roots are more likely to keep a crown green than to provide stability. Roots of palms and roots initiated from cuttings on vegetatively propagated trees are adventitious.

Structural Roots

Although they are not a distinct type of root, structural roots are large, woody roots near the trunk that provide anchorage and support. These roots are characterized by secondary thickening (xylem growth) and relatively large diameters. To varying extents, lateral, oblique, sinker, and tap roots all serve to anchor or support the tree crown and, therefore, can be considered structural roots.

Root Systems: Structure and Distribution

Hardwoods (angiosperms) and conifers (gymnosperms) — Based on the relative dominance of tap, lateral, and oblique roots, root systems for hardwoods and conifers have been classified into three groups (Figure 3):

- Tap root systems are composed of a prominent tap root but also have varying numbers of lateral roots. They may or may not possess oblique and sinker roots. For many species, the tap root is prominent only in seedlings and has a diminishing role as the tree matures.
- Heart root systems consist of a relatively high proportion of oblique roots and tend to develop deeper in the soil profile compared to lateral root systems. They are called heart root systems because oblique roots are also known as heart roots.
- Lateral root systems are dominated by lateral roots occurring largely near the soil surface and lack predominant tap and oblique roots.

Species inherently develop a particular type of root system; some tend to develop lateral systems, while others develop heart root or tap root systems. For species native to temperate, semitropical, and tropical climate zones, lateral root systems generally are more common than heart root or tap root systems. For species native to Mediterranean, semiarid, and arid climate zones, heart root systems generally are more common than lateral or tap root systems. Of the three types of root systems, tap root systems are least common.

Regardless of genetics, the overall spread and depth of an individual tree's root system is greatly influenced by the soil environment. A species that typically develops a heart root or tap root system in deep, uniform soils may develop a lateral root system in shallower soils in which the growth of oblique roots is restricted.

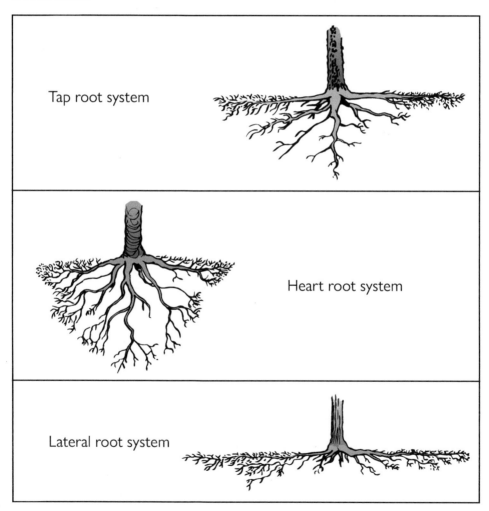

Figure 3. Root systems have been classified into three groups: tap root systems, heart root systems, and lateral root systems. Soil conditions strongly influence root system development.

Soil oxygen naturally diminishes with depth, so trees have fewer roots below 4 ft (1.2 m). In addition, a high groundwater table will force roots to grow shallower, whereas a deep groundwater table does not limit downward root growth.

Roots systems are naturally wide spreading. Lateral roots commonly grow well beyond the drip line of the crown, often two to three times the radius of the crown if the soil is not restricted. However, infrastructure and soil that restricts growth can limit the development of roots. In some cases, root development may be limited on one side of the tree. It should not be assumed that lateral root development is symmetrical or uniform around the trunk.

Tree roots can grow to great depths, but depth is usually restricted by soil conditions. High **water tables** and compacted subsurface layers, such as **hardpans**, clay layers, and bedrock, can restrict penetration of oblique, sinker, and tap roots. If cracks or fissures occur in underlying rock or hardpan layers, however, roots may penetrate and grow to substantial depths. So while roots have been found at depths more than 200 ft (60 m), most tree roots are found in the upper 4 ft (1.2 m) and most fine roots are found in the upper 6 in (15 cm) in humid climates.

Palms—Palm (*Arecaceae* spp.) root systems are composed of numerous slender, fibrous, primary roots that arise and grow independently of one another from the **root initiation zone (RIZ)** at the base of the trunk (Figure 4). Because all palm roots arise from the trunk, they are considered to be adventitious. Palm roots lack a mechanism for secondary growth, so they do not increase in diameter after being formed. However, in some instances, they can resprout and grow if cut or damaged.

The RIZ is typically at or near the soil line but can extend several feet (one meter or more) above ground. Depending on the climate (temperature, humidity, and precipitation) and, to some extent, the substrate (accumulation of leaf litter around the trunk), roots emerging from the RIZ above the soil line may not grow into the soil, particularly in arid climates and/or where leaf litter is removed, such as in a maintained landscape. Essentially, they are air pruned by low humidity and appear as short root initials. In more humid climates, roots emerging from the RIZ of some species may grow through the air and then into the ground.

Most palm roots are found in the upper foot (30 cm) of soil and may grow out many feet (meters) from the trunk. Primary roots typically branch into an extensive network of secondary and tertiary roots (called a **root mat**) around the base of the trunk and spread outward for a few feet (about 1 m). However, under optimal growing conditions, palm roots can grow considerable distances. For example, in well-irrigated, light, sandy soil, roots of *Phoenix dactylifera* have been reported to extend over 10 ft (3 m) deep and 100 ft (30 m) from the trunk.

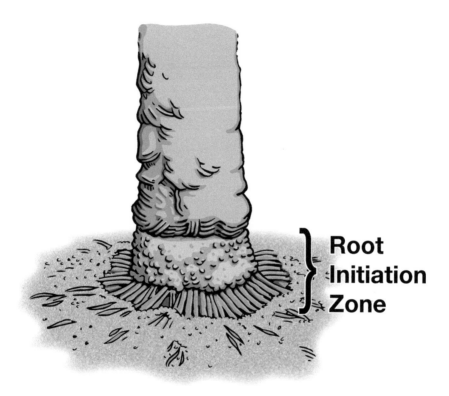

} **Root**
} **Initiation**
} **Zone**

Figure 4. The palm root system is composed of numerous, slender, tubelike, fibrous roots that arise and grow from the root initiation zone (RIZ) at the base of the trunk. Because all palm roots arise from the trunk, they are considered to be adventitious. Although the majority of the RIZ is above ground, it can extend below ground as well.

3. Root Inspection

Roots and the root flare may be located and inspected[1] for a number of reasons, including to diagnose a problem, prepare for root pruning or construction, or perform an advanced **tree risk assessment**. There are several ways to locate roots prior to excavation, including probing into the soil to find roots and the use of **ground-penetrating radar (GPR)**. To find roots at a predetermined location, such as near the trunk or in advance of construction, soil excavation may be the simplest method to locate the roots for inspection. Excavations range from small scale (e.g., a small hole to make sure that no roots will be damaged when a deck footing is installed) to large scale (e.g., a preconstruction excavation around a large tree to determine the location of large structural roots). The reason for conducting the excavation and inspection will determine the location and depth of the excavation.

Root collar excavation (RCX) is the process of removing mulch or soil covering the root collar and the uppermost lateral roots. The **root collar** (root flare or trunk flare) is the transition zone from trunk to roots. This area should be distinct and visible. If the root collar area is covered with mulch, soil, or ground-cover plants, this area cannot be visually inspected. Soil and mulch can retain high levels of moisture on the trunk that may soften the bark and allow for easier entry of certain fungal pathogens. Furthermore, like all aboveground plant tissues, root collars require the exchange of oxygen and carbon dioxide. When root collars are covered with mulch and/or soil, gas exchange can be reduced. This can lead to stress within the tree, and boring insects may be attracted to the tree. Some boring insects take advantage of the soil or mulch cover to attack the tree more easily.

As a general practice, mulch and ground-cover plants that obstruct the view of the root collar area should be kept back a distance of at least 1 ft (30 cm) from the trunk.

Locating Roots

There are several tools and techniques that can be used to locate lateral roots near the trunk, an individual root away from the trunk, or all of the roots in a

---

1 A visual examination of the root system shall not be considered a tree risk assessment unless explicitly stated in the scope of work.

defined soil area. As with all digging, the area should be inspected and marked for underground electric wires, gas pipes, and other utilities prior to digging.

Excavation by hand, high-pressure air, or water tools can be effective ways to locate and expose roots but may be difficult and time consuming, and care must be taken to minimize damage to roots. Air or water excavation can rapidly remove soil around roots and buried structures, such as irrigation pipes or utilities, with minimal injury. Structural roots can be traced from the trunk to the area of concern, or the area can be directly sampled. Exploratory trenches can be dug across root systems to locate roots and assess number, size, depth, and distance from the trunk. This technique is useful when evaluating potential impacts to root systems from construction activities.

A stiff rod, such as a tile probe or survey pin (Figure 5), can be pushed into low-density soil to locate larger roots that will stop the movement of the probe tip. Some practice is required to distinguish the feel of roots compared to rocks or dense soil.

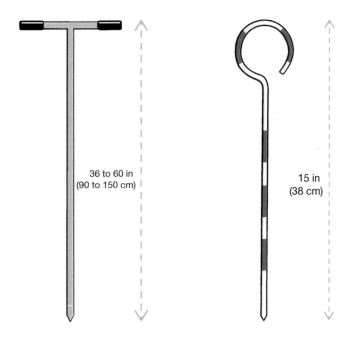

36 to 60 in
(90 to 150 cm)

15 in
(38 cm)

Figure 5: Tile probe (left) and survey pin (right).

GPR and signal processing software can be used to detect roots and other features under soil, concrete, and asphalt. Under ideal conditions, they can locate roots with diameters as small as 0.4 inches (1 cm) and as deep as 3 ft (1 m). GPR is limited by soil textures and moisture content. Maps of soil suitability for the use of GPR can be found for the United States on the Natural Resources Conservation Service website.

Often companies that conduct utility location services provide GPR inspections. A skilled operator is required to interpret data and identify the location of tree roots.

Root Excavation and Examination

There are three basic methods of removing soil from around roots or the root collar to allow for root locating, inspection, pruning, or other work: manual excavation, air (pneumatic) excavation, and water (hydraulic) excavation.

Preparation for Excavation

Mulch, turf, or other ground cover may need to be removed from the excavation area prior to excavation. Mulch is usually raked to one side or into a pile for removal from the site or replacement after the inspection is complete. Turf can be removed with a shovel if the project is small or a sod cutter if the project is large. The turf may also be killed with a nonpersistent herbicide weeks prior to excavation to make manual removal easier.

A few fine tree roots that interfere with the excavation can usually be removed without seriously damaging tree health. Larger roots (greater than 2 in [5 cm] in diameter) should be retained when possible.

With manual and air excavation, soil moisture level will greatly affect the ease of digging or removal of the soil. For hand digging, the soil moisture should be between the wilt point and field capacity.[2] With air excavation, soil moisture should be near field capacity. If dust is being generated, the soil is too dry. During dry periods, irrigation should be applied prior to excavation. In many cases, starting irrigation days before the excavation will allow the water time to percolate to the depth of excavation.

---

2 See Scharenbroch and Smiley 2021.

On sites with a history of soil contamination, excavation should be avoided unless the arborist has the assistance of a professional knowledgeable in legally working in such conditions.

Manual Excavation

Manual excavation involves carefully removing soil using shovels, trowels, gloved hands, and/or brushes. Bark that has been covered with soil may be soft and easily damaged by metal tools, especially on species with thin bark. The excavation can start with a spade to remove larger volumes of soil, but a smaller tool, such as a trowel, should be used as the excavation gets closer to roots. The bark can be cleaned with a stiff-bristled brush (not a wire brush) if needed.

Air (pneumatic) Excavation

Air excavation uses high-pressure air tools designed for moving soil (Figure 6). These tools require both high pressure and large volumes of air. To generate this, a trailered or truck-mounted compressor capable of generating 100 pounds/in^2 (76 bars) of pressure and 135 ft^3/min (3.8 m^3/min) of volume is needed.

The technician should hold the tool at about a 45° to 90° angle to the surface to rapidly move the soil. The lower the angle of the tool, the greater the distance the soil will be moved. When the tool is pointed straight down (90° angle), it can cut to a greater depth, and the soil can be blown straight upward at the operator. The nozzle should be kept several inches from the bark to avoid damage, especially on thin-barked species in the spring. Uplifted soil can be scattered into the surrounding landscape or collected against a fabric or wood barrier so that it can be returned to or removed from the site.

It is very time consuming to air excavate to soil depths greater than 6 in (15 cm). If greater excavations depths are required, a larger-volume air tool and larger compressor may be used, or a mechanical excavator, such as a backhoe, may be used in conjunction with an air-excavation tool.

It is important that the technician using a high-pressure air tool wear adequate personal protective equipment (PPE), including both safety glasses and a face shield, both ear plugs and earmuffs, a hard hat, gloves, boots, a long-sleeved shirt, and long pants. If dust is generated during the operation, a dust mask

Figure 6. Air (pneumatic) excavation uses high-pressure, large-volume air tools designed for soil tilling or removal.

that filters silica dust is required. Additional personal protection, including a neck protector and coveralls, is recommended. If fire ants (*Solenopsis*) or other stinging insects are present in the area, they should be treated ahead of time, and clothing leg, sleeve, and neck openings of equipment should be sealed.

High-pressure air can propel rocks some distance, so nearby windows, cars, and structures should be protected with wood barriers or fabric tarps. Observers should be kept a safe distance from the work. If dust is generated, nearby structures may need to be cleaned when the excavation is finished.

Water (Hydraulic) Excavation

Hydraulic excavation uses pressurized water to break up and move soil from the area to be inspected. Hydraulic and hydrovac tools create much less dust than air tools. Pressurized water can come from a pressure washer, high-volume tree sprayer, or a large-diameter hose. High-pressure water from any of these devices can rapidly move soil from around roots. Water from a pressure washer can often break up soil that an air excavator cannot penetrate. However, high pressure water can also easily remove bark from tree roots causing injury. If a pressure washer is used, the nozzle should be

Most soil management work sites have strict requirements for personal protective equipment (PPE) that must be worn.

Basic equipment for all work sites typically includes:

- Hard hat
- Eye protection
- High-visibility clothing
- Long-sleeved shirt and long pants
- Work boots and socks

With manual soil excavations, additional PPE includes:

- Face shield and/or safety glasses
- Work gloves
- Knee pads

With high-pressure air excavations, additional PPE includes:

- Double hearing protection (ear plugs and muffs)
- Eye and face protection (safety glasses and face shield)
- Respirator, if dust is present (for protection against silica and other dust)
- Neck protection (to reduce dust under clothing)
- Sealing of collar, wrists, and ankles (for stinging pests)

With water excavations, additional PPE includes:

- Eye and face protection (safety glasses and face shield)
- Hearing protection (ear plugs, earmuffs, or both, depending on sound level)
- Rain gear
- Rubber boots

kept at least 1 ft (30 cm) from roots. If root injury is observed, the nozzle should be moved farther from the roots.

Another limitation of hydraulic excavation is the disposal of the water and mud generated during excavation. If there is no area for the water and mud to flow away from the excavation area, a vacuum system can be used to pull the slurry of water and soil away into a large tank mounted on a truck or trailer. Most hydraulic excavation contractors have equipment that includes a vacuum to collect the slurry.

As with air excavation, it is important that the technician using a high-pressure water tool have adequate personal protective equipment, including long-sleeved shirt, safety glasses, face shield, ear plugs or earmuffs, a hard hat, gloves, rubber boots, and rain gear.

Root Collar Excavation (RCX)

As with all arboriculture services, the objective of the RCX should be defined in advance so the area that will be excavated (i.e., location, width, and depth) and tools to be used can be determined. The most common objectives for RCX are to expose the lower trunk and root collar. This is done to allow inspection, tree injection, or the bark to dry, which may limit some diseases.

Extent of Excavation

Excavations should be deep enough to expose the top of the uppermost lateral roots and associated buttressing. However, if the tree trunk has been buried for many years or decades with more than 1.5 to 2 ft (45 to 60 cm) of soil, it is possible that soil next to the trunk is providing support for the tree. When excavation exceeds that depth, an advanced risk assessment may be warranted to determine if there is significant root decay. If significant decay is present and the risk is unacceptable, risk mitigation, such as tree removal, may be necessary. When the decay analysis or mitigation cannot be completed on a timely basis, it is best to refill the excavation until the work can be completed. This additional, noncompacted soil may not have the ability to support the tree.

The width of the excavation will be determined by the objective. The excavation may only need to be several inches (centimeters) wide if it is for a quick inspection before climbing the tree. When a more thorough inspection or advanced risk assessment is planned, an excavation depth of 1 ft (30 cm) or deeper may be needed.

When the intent is to permanently expose the root collar, the excavation should gradually slope to the existing grade. A 3:1 (run:rise) slope or less is preferred (Figure 7). A tree well may be needed if space is not available for a gradual slope.

If topography allows, a drainage trench or pipe may aid in keeping water from collecting in tree wells or excavations with steeper slopes. If the excavation is 6 in (15 cm) or deeper and relatively small diameter, it can be filled with rounded (river) rock. The rock has limited water-holding capacity and a relatively flat soil surface that may look better and be less of a tripping hazard.

After excavating, the newly exposed soil surface should be covered with mulch whenever possible. For thin-barked species excavated in the late summer or fall, covering newly exposed root bark with a layer of wood chip mulch can lessen the chance of **sunburn** and excessive root drying.

Potential Problems

Conditions that may be present on the lower trunk or root flare that can indicate problems with the root system include cut, severed, decayed, or otherwise damaged roots; missing roots; dead or decayed trunk wood; dead, unusual, wounded, or missing bark; oozing sap; sharp growth angles; girdling roots, rope, wire, or straps; unusual root flare swelling; the fusing together of structural roots; and the presence of adventitious roots or fungal **fruiting bodies**. The presence of root decay and the loss of roots by other means may result in a higher likelihood of failure. Positive indicators of decay include cavity openings, fungal fruiting bodies, and/or the presence of carpenter ants. Any of these conditions may warrant an advanced tree risk assessment (see Appendix 2).

Girdling is the term used to describe roots, straps, wires, ropes, or other materials that encircle, confine, or limit the growth of the trunk or other roots. **Stem girdling roots (SGRs)** are roots that grow around or across the trunk or major lateral roots. Girdling can reduce sap flow, which can lead to tree decline or death. In more severe cases, the reduction of trunk growth can create a structural weakness and even lead to tree failure. Girdling is often identified during an RCX. Information on removing girdling roots can be found in the next section of this BMP.

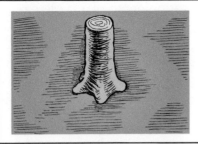

a. When the lower trunk or buttress roots are covered with soil, mulch, or other materials, a root collar excavation should be recommended.

b. Root excavations should be deep enough to expose the top of the uppermost lateral roots and associated buttressing.

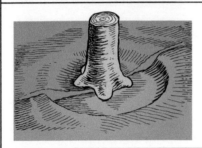

c. If permanently exposing the root collar, the grade should gradually slope to the existing grade; a 10° or less angle is preferred.

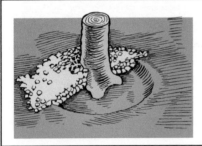

d. If excavation is 6 in (15 cm) or deeper, it can be filled with rounded (river) rock to allow rapid drainage.

e. For thin-barked species excavated in late summer or fall, cover newly exposed bark with a layer of wood chip mulch to avoid sunscalding and drying.

Figure 7. Root collar excavation (RCX) considerations.

4. Root Pruning

Ideally, tree roots should not be cut when there are other options for management. Roots are typically pruned when they interfere with existing or proposed infrastructure, to limit the spread of vascular disease, or to correct defects that affect tree health or stability. Infrastructure damage includes lifting of sidewalks, creating tripping hazards or limiting access; damaging building or wall foundations; plugging sewer pipes; and disrupting underground utilities. Much root cutting occurs on construction sites during excavation for foundations, installation of underground utilities, and changes to the grade. The spread of vascular diseases, such as oak wilt and Dutch elm disease, can be limited when root connections between adjacent trees are cut. Tree health and stability concerns include assessment of root decay, stem girdling roots, and circling roots.

The consequences of root pruning have not been well studied. Small-diameter root cuts and damage that is limited to root sapwood are thought to compartmentalize well and do not usually lead to extensive decay. When larger roots are cut and **heartwood** is exposed, decay is more likely to develop. The resulting decay can affect root strength years or decades later in temperate climates. Other factors that can affect decay spread are tree and fungus species, the distance of root cuts from the trunk, and soil moisture and temperature.

There are two general methods used for cutting roots. First is **selective root pruning**, which involves locating and exposing roots, then making targeted pruning cuts. The second is **nonselective root cutting**, which involves mechanical excavating or **trenching** the soil along a predetermined line and indiscriminately severing the roots.

Both selective root pruning and nonselective cutting can cause great harm to a tree, especially if key structural roots are affected. Damage may reduce tree health and/or structural stability. To minimize tree health impacts, when roots must be pruned, they should be cut as far from the trunk as is practical.

In some situations, an alternative to cutting through the entire root may be to shave the top of the root. While not a preferred option, root shaving is occasionally done when roots are lifting pavement and new pavement needs to be installed above the offending roots. If roots are to be shaved, the amount of wood removed should be kept to a minimum to achieve the goal, but no more than one-third of the diameter of the root should be removed. Shaving into heartwood and creating sharp angle cuts should be avoided. Root shaving is not a permanent solution to pavement lifting. Future radial growth of the root and woundwood can result in the reoccurrence of lifting. A layer of foam may be installed over the top of the shaved root to increase the time before lifting reoccurs. While root shaving may be less damaging than root cutting, decay fungi may infect these wounds.

Objectives of root pruning or nonselective cutting should be determined with the client and stated in the scope of work or contract. Common objectives include mitigation of root defects (e.g., SGRs), preparing for soil excavation, and removing roots to minimize infrastructure damage.

Selective Root Pruning vs. Nonselective Root Cutting

Selective root pruning starts with soil excavation and root exposure, followed by the cutting of individual roots. Excavation prior to root pruning allows the arborist to examine the roots and determine the best location to make pruning cuts, preferably beyond (distal to) sinker roots or outside root branch unions (Figure 8). This can make it possible to cut fewer roots or to make several smaller cuts instead of a single larger-diameter cut. Tools used should be selected based on the root diameter and location. They include hand pruners (secateurs), chisels, loppers, hand saws, reciprocating saws, oscillating saws, and small chain saws.

Just as flush cutting branches is not an acceptable practice, a pruning cut that removes a root at its point of origin should not cut into the parent root. Root pruning cuts should be made cleanly using a sharp tool appropriate for the root diameter, leaving a clean cut that is perpendicular to the direction of growth, with the bark intact.

Nonselective root cutting is less targeted than selective root pruning. Usually, root cutting is the result of trenching or soil excavation that does not intentionally target tree roots. Rather, it is done to install pipes or wires in a trench, to change soil grade for construction, or for sidewalk or pavement removal or replacement. Unfortunately, most equipment operators are not aware of the tree damage being inflicted during these operations. However, once trained, a capable excavator operator can minimize root damage.

Figure 8. Selective root pruning consists of soil excavation prior to root pruning to determine the best places to make cuts (right). Nonselective root cutting is less targeted, usually causing root damage as the result of trenching or soil excavation that does not intentionally target tree roots (left).

Regardless of the reason for nonselective root cutting, it is better to use specifically designed mechanical root-pruning tools (e.g., Vermeer, Imants, or Dosko root pruners) to provide moderately clean root cuts. When tools not specifically designed for root cutting, such as trenchers, excavators, and backhoes, are used, they result in torn, splintered, and crushed roots; thus, they are the least preferred. Cutting a line with a root pruner on the tree side of the excavation line prior to excavation can limit this type of damage.

If roots are not cut prior to excavation, any exposed root ends over 1 in (2.5 cm) in diameter should be pruned beyond the damaged area rather than left torn or crushed. The final root cut should result in a flat surface with the adjacent bark firmly attached. Exposed roots should be shaded and kept moist, such as by using moist burlap.

Stem Girdling Roots

Stem girdling roots (SGRs) are roots that grow around or across the base of the trunk (Figure 9). They often originate inside a nursery container when the stem is buried and roots grow to the container wall, then turn and continue growing in a circular orientation. If not eliminated at planting, these roots often persist after installation in the landscape. SGRs have also been associated with excessive soil over the root system in the root collar area. SGRs can originate as existing nearly perpendicular branches of radial lateral roots whose growth increases after the radial root is cut (similar to a lateral branch growth increasing when the terminal is cut). Certain species seem to be naturally prone to developing girdling roots (e.g., maples [*Acer* spp.], hackberry [*Celtis* spp.], linden [*Tilia* spp.], elms [*Ulmus* spp.], and *Zelkovas* spp.). SGRs are so common on Norway maples (*Acer platanoides*) that fewer are being planted.

SGRs will typically cause a gradual decline in health, though they can lead to sudden failures during wind-loading events. Aboveground decline symptoms

Figure 9. Girdling is the term used to describe roots that encircle, confine, or limit the growth of the trunk or other root. Stem girdling roots (SGRs) are roots that girdle the base of the trunk.

of SGRs include small leaves, early autumn color, gradual reduction of terminal growth, dieback of branches in sections of the canopy, and partial or total absence of a root flare. SGRs can restrict vascular transport by constricting phloem tissue and sapwood.

The treatment for SGRs is selective pruning of the offending roots. Some amount of root collar excavation (RCX) may be necessary to expose the SGRs. Pruning is commonly done with loppers, chisels, oscillating saws, hand saws, or small chain saws. Roots should be cut on both sides of the area being girdled. Roots that encircle or fully girdle the trunk should be removed before they are engulfed by trunk tissue if possible. Grafting between roots and trunk tissue is rare because the bark on both root and trunk creates a barrier between the cambium layers. When pruning a girdling root, care should be taken not to damage trunk tissue.

Removal of SGRs results in the loss of a portion of the root system and a corresponding reduction of water and nutrient supply to the crown. As a general rule, if the girdling root is more than one-third of the diameter of the stem, its removal will impact tree health and can even result in whole tree mortality. Therefore, if one or more large girdling roots are present, consider progressive root pruning over a specified period of time. This may involve starting with a notch cut one-third to one-half of the way through a girdling root to slow its growth and to relieve the pressure on stem tissues. After a year or more, the notch may be enlarged to further slow the root growth or the root can be entirely severed.

Although there is the potential for SGR removal to induce temporary physiological stress, the condition of the tree can improve over time as the vascular constriction is overcome with the addition of new tissue. Fertilization and crown pruning are not substitutes for SGR removal. If stem tissue remains in contact with soil after SGR removal, SGRs can recur. Maintaining a soil- and mulch-free root collar area will minimize the growth of a new SGR.

Long-Term Effects of Root Pruning

Root pruning reduces the root system's capacity to absorb water and nutrients, which can create water stress and initiate tree decline. Root loss can impact tree vitality due to a loss of stored energy and hormone synthesis. The crown can respond with less growth or, in more severe cases, branch mortality. Older trees may be more severely affected than established younger trees.

Root loss can be considered temporary when cut roots are able to regenerate and eventually replace lost root function. However, species vary in their ability to recover from such temporary root loss. For instance, post oaks (*Quercus stellata*) are notorious for their poor recovery from this type of injury, while many species of *Ulmus, Platanus,* and *Robinia* can respond well to root injury.

If root space is permanently lost (e.g., from lowering the grade or construction of a structure or nonporous pavement in the root zone) after root pruning, then the root system cannot be replaced in that area, and stress and stability concerns may never be overcome.

Consequences of Root Pruning on Tree Health and Stability

When root cuts are necessary, they should be as far from the trunk as possible. Tree response to root cuts is dependent on tree species, age, condition, root configuration, and soil characteristics, including the presence of underground root obstructions.

Cutting roots closer than six times diameter at breast height (**DBH**) on one side of the tree can cause sustained and chronic water-stress symptoms in some species (Figure 10). This stress in turn can lead to other tree health problems, such as increased susceptibility to pests and diseases, drought, or other environmental pressures.

When cuts are made closer to the trunk, stability and health may be compromised and should therefore be avoided. Tree stability has been found to be compromised on some species when cuts are made within three times the trunk diameter from the trunk.

For most species, when roots are cut closer than one- to one-and-a-half times the DBH distance from the trunk, a serious reduction in stability can occur and long-term health and survival will be impacted. Should large roots be cut that close to the trunk, it may be better to remove the tree rather than preserve it. If the tree is retained, monitor the structural stability, and maintain a safe zone around the tree. Maintain tree health with good arboricultural practices, such as additional watering and soil amending, to improve root health.

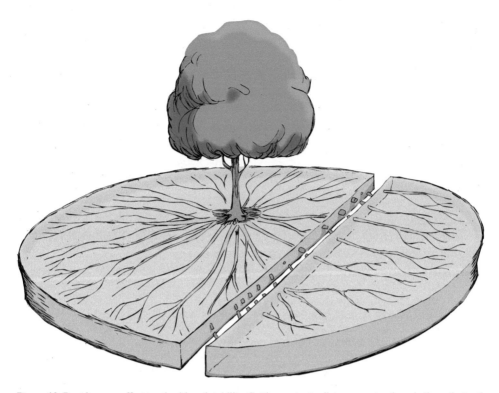

Figure 10. Root loss can affect tree health and stability. Cutting roots at a distance greater than six times the trunk diameter (DBH) minimizes the likelihood of affecting both health and stability. At this distance, approximately 25 percent of the root system would be lost. Since many landscape trees do not have the even distribution of roots shown in this illustration, the percentage cut at this distance may be more or less than calculated.

New Root Growth

When woody roots are cut, numerous adventitious roots may be initiated at, or just behind, the cut surface. In unrestricted areas, these roots typically elongate in the same direction as the original root. The rate of growth is affected by the environment and available resources from the tree. Annual root extension depends on species, soil moisture, soil density, and temperature. For example, in the upper midwestern United States (USDA Hardiness Zone 5, min. temperatures to -20 °F /-29 °C), with moderate summers and frozen soils in winter, typical annual root elongation is about 18 in (45 cm), and in a subtropical climate (USDA Hardiness Zone 9, min. temperatures to 20 °F /-7 °C), annual root growth is 6 ft (2 m) or more. Root growth rates can also depend on tree species. The number of years required to replace lost roots can be calculated as the estimated length of roots lost divided by the estimated annual growth extension in that hardiness zone. Trees with

The **tree protection zone (TPZ)** is the area within which certain activities are prohibited or restricted to prevent or minimize potential injury to designated trees, especially during construction or development.

Defining the TPZ is often a two-step process. The arborist often starts with a **calculated TPZ**. As the project progresses, the size and shape of the TPZ may need to be adjusted to identify the **specified TPZ** and where a TPZ barrier will be located.

A TPZ can be calculated using the trunk diameter, the species tolerance to construction, and the age-class of the tree (Table 1). With this method, the DBH is multiplied by a factor of 6 to 18, depending on the tree age and species' construction tolerance, to calculate the radius of the TPZ.

Table 1. Guidelines for calculating tree protection zone radius for trees in good condition (adapted from Matheny and Clark 2023). To use this table, determine the TPZ multiplication factor based on the species tolerance to construction damage and relative tree age. That number (TPZ multiplication factor) is then multiplied by the tree trunk diameter (DBH). The result is the radius of the TPZ in the same units used to measure DBH. That number is usually converted to feet or meters.

Species Tolerance to Construction Damage	Relative Tree Age*	Multiplication Factor
High	Young or semimature	6
	Mature	8
	Old	12
Medium	Young or semimature	8
	Mature	12
	Old	15
Low	Young or semimature	12
	Mature	15
	Old	18

*Young to semimature = less than 40 percent life expectancy; mature = 40 to 80 percent life expectancy; old = greater than 80 percent life expectancy.

A TPZ should be specified based on site-specific conditions. The actual location of tree protection barriers may deviate from the calculated TPZ; this is the specified TPZ. The arborist determines the specified TPZ through on-site evaluation.

damaged root systems usually benefit from supplemental irrigation and mulch over the remaining roots during periods of drought, until the lost root function is replaced.

Cut palm roots frequently sprout and branch into a network of roots. In tropical regions where temperatures, humidity, and moisture are not limiting, palm roots emerge and grow year round, sometimes in distinct flushes. For example, in regions with distinct growing seasons, such as the southwestern United States, roots grow mostly during the warmer months and when there is adequate rain or irrigation water.

Root Growth Stimulants

Many kinds of root-stimulating products have been marketed over the years. Possible treatments include vitamin compounds, seaweed extracts, growth hormones, plant growth regulators, **auxin**, carbohydrates, and mycorrhizal fungi.

The effectiveness of many of these products in stimulating root growth has not been consistently shown in landscape situations or by research. If testing the products on your own, be sure to include untreated plants for a comparison to judge whether they are really effective. Usually, other cultural treatments, such as mulching, organic matter incorporation, and fertilization, can provide greater benefits.

Care of Root Pruned Trees

Trees that have sustained root loss should be monitored regularly for symptoms of stress, insects, pathogens, and decline. Monitoring should continue for up to five years because visible symptoms of stress may not develop right away. If root loss occurs while the tree is in leaf, signs of water stress, such as early seasonal leaf color change, defoliation, dull or drooping leaves and branch tips, and scorched leaf margins, may develop in the same season. Other symptoms of stress, such as reduced twig elongation and leaf size, will not be evident until the next growing season. Trees responding to root loss will often leaf out late, develop open and sparse canopies, have atypically sized leaves, and may show premature leaf loss.

Following root pruning, cultural practices that minimize stress should be implemented to avoid secondary problems and promote root development.

Most importantly, soil should be kept moist (but not saturated) throughout the root zone. More frequent irrigation might be needed during hot, dry periods. Eliminating turfgrass and applying a 2 to 4 in (5 to 10 cm) layer of organic mulch will help to reduce competition for soil moisture and minimize evaporative water loss.

If a nutrient deficiency is suspected, a soil or foliar sample should be collected and analyzed before fertilizer is applied.[3] In the absence of a deficiency, fertilization will not substantially increase root development.

In cases of extreme root loss, tree removal or tree height reduction may reduce the likelihood of root-related whole tree failure. If branch dieback is evident, pruning may be required. Advanced root or stability assessment should be recommended when appropriate (Appendix 2).

---

3 *See* Smiley et al. 2020.

5. Minimizing Conflicts with Infrastructure

Infrastructure that may be damaged by tree roots includes sidewalks, footpaths, driveways, curbs, gutters, pavement, water lines, sewer pipes, buried utilities, and foundations. When the root flare or tree roots contact these elements, they can be lifted, cracked, displaced, or otherwise damaged. In addition, roots can grow through faulty joints or cracks in foundations and sewer pipes, causing damage or obstructions.

Repairing infrastructure damage is usually costly and often results in requests for tree removal. Therefore, minimizing the potential for damage is a key management objective for tree care professionals. Often this is simply a matter of growing the right tree in the right place for the right purpose. This section presents information on infrastructure damage and strategies to minimize conflicts.

Infrastructure Position and Associated Damage

Infrastructure can be classified by position, being either at the soil surface or beneath it (subsurface). Surface infrastructure includes sidewalks, curbs, gutters, pavements, and their underlying compacted **base layer**, if present. Subsurface infrastructure addressed here includes sewer pipes, water lines, utilities, and building foundations.

Surface Infrastructure: Sidewalks, Curbs, Gutters, and Pavement

Infrastructure damage is commonly associated with large trees in restricted planting spaces. While damage is greatly reduced by increasing the distance between trees and infrastructure, optimal distances are often difficult to achieve in many urban locations. The potential for conflicts between trees and infrastructure is high when one or more of the following factors are present:

- Fast-growing species that are large at maturity
- Species with an inherently shallow rooting characteristic
- Distance between the tree and infrastructure is less than 6 ft (2 m)
- Trees planted in restricted soil volumes, such as compacted or shallow soils

- Limited or no base materials exist beneath sidewalks or pavements (e.g., pavement is installed directly on the soil rather than on a layer of compacted gravel).

When infrastructure such as sidewalks or pavement is laid on a compacted soil base, roots may grow between the structure and the soil. Moisture level is relatively high under the pavement because the material prevents evaporation, and condensation can occur on the underside as pavement is heated and then cools. Natural expansion and contraction of soil due to wetting/drying or freezing/thawing, can also create an air gap under the pavement and encourage root growth. As roots grow in diameter, they can eventually lift and crack the sidewalk.

Lateral roots grow horizontally and principally develop near the soil surface. As a result, they often conflict with nearby surface infrastructure (e.g., pavement or sidewalks). In addition, if the trunk is close to the infrastructure, the developing root flare can cause damage.

Certain species are prone to developing a large number of lateral roots at the soil surface (e.g., *Liquidambar styraciflua, Pinus pinea,* and *Populus* spp.) and have a higher potential for causing damage than species prone to developing deeper roots. Soils that restrict the downward development of roots (for example, soils with compacted layers below the surface or shallow water tables) promote shallow root development. Shallow root development associated with restrictive soils can occur even in species that are noted for developing deep roots (e.g., *Quercus* spp. *and Juglans* spp.).

Generally, the fibrous, adventitious nature of palm root systems causes less damage compared to root systems from hardwoods and conifers. However, in some instances, the sheer number of roots and the size of the expanding root mat of palms are sufficient to damage infrastructure.

Species that develop a prominent root flare (e.g., *Olea europaea, Acer saccharinum,* and *Cinnamomum camphora*), can damage infrastructure near the trunk. Frequently, this occurs when a species with a large flare is planted too close to a sidewalk or foundation. As the flare enlarges, it can cause nearby infrastructure to be displaced.

Subsurface Infrastructure: Sewer Pipes and Foundations

Tree root intrusion into sewer pipes can be a substantial problem, especially in smaller and older pipes. Tree roots rarely initiate new damage to sewer pipes, but they take advantage of breaks, leaks, displaced pipes, and loose joints, proliferating rapidly once inside the moist, nutrient-rich environment (Figure 11).

Roots tend to follow utility trench installation and many can develop around the utility pipes. The interface between the pipe surface and the surrounding soil offers less resistance to penetration, thus requiring less energy for root growth and exploration for water and nutrition acquisition. These situations ultimately provide a path for root growth immediately in proximity to any joint or gap in the pipe system.

Because sewer pipes are usually located lower in the soil profile relative to sidewalks and pavements, sinker and oblique roots are more likely than lateral roots to be associated with intrusion. Fine roots at the end of these roots are small enough to penetrate cracks in pipes or damaged joints.

Although older clay and concrete pipes without rubber gaskets in the joints (pipe unions) have the least resistance to root intrusion, newer PVC and concrete pipes with gaskets also can be penetrated. Roots have been reported to grow into pipes relatively quickly. Although certain tree species, such

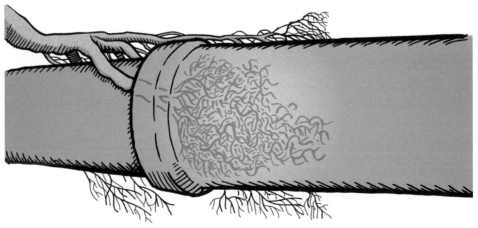

Figure 11. Tree root intrusion into sanitary sewer systems can be a substantial problem, especially in smaller and older pipes. Tree roots rarely initiate new damage to sewer pipes, but they take advantage of breaks, leaks, displaced pipes, and loose joints, proliferating rapidly once inside the moist, nutrient-rich environment.

as poplar (*Populus* spp.), willow (*Salix* spp.), melaleuca (*Melaleuca* spp.), and eucalyptus (*Eucalyptus* spp.), have been reported to have a high potential to intrude into sewer pipes, research has found that the roots of a wide range of species grow into sewer pipes.

The position of the tree relative to the type, depth, and location of sewers is an important factor affecting root intrusion. In general, trees with relatively large crowns and naturally deeper roots growing close to sewer lines have a higher potential to intrude than trees with small crowns growing farther away.

Foundations

Roots generally will not penetrate sound concrete foundations or cause deterioration of concrete. Roots can enter existing cracks in foundations or penetrate deteriorated mortar, especially if soil moisture is high near the foundation. As the roots grow and enlarge in diameter, they cause the cracks or joints to expand. With shallow or slab foundations, roots can grow below the concrete and lift the foundation as they increase in diameter.

Roots contribute indirectly to foundation damage in areas with soils that have a high shrink–swell capacity. Certain types of clay soils (reactive clays) with high shrink-swell potential, such as montmorillonite and bentonite, naturally shrink when dry and swell when wet. Trees can contribute to soil-moisture depletion (via transpiration), causing the soil to shrink and potentially causing the building foundation to settle and crack. In some cases, rainfall can cause soil to expand, causing foundations to heave. Poorly designed, undersized, inadequately reinforced, and/or deteriorating foundations are most susceptible to this type of damage.

Minimizing Conflicts: Strategies, Objectives, and Practice

Strategies to reduce conflicts between tree roots and infrastructure can be classified as being either preventive or remedial. **Preventive strategies** are used to avoid or minimize future conflicts. **Remedial strategies** are employed when infrastructure damage has occurred and attempts are made to repair damage or minimize further damage. For established trees that are large enough to cause damage, strategies are largely remedial. For newly planted trees, strategies are mainly preventive.

For both established and newly planted trees, strategies can be further classified based on the focus of the action: the tree itself, the infrastructure element, or the soil environment. Tree-based strategies include species selection and root pruning, while infrastructure-based strategies include enlarging planting spaces or using alternatives to concrete. Soil-based strategies focus on modifications that reduce the potential for root contact with infrastructure, with common examples including root barriers, supported pavement systems (e.g., modular cells and structural soils), and deep cultivation of soil.

All strategies have limitations. Some are suitable for certain locations and circumstances, while others are not. In some cases, multiple strategies are appropriate. For example, where sidewalk damage has been caused by an established tree, a combination of root pruning, sidewalk realignment to provide more space, and the installation of a linear root barrier may be the best approach. For newly planted trees, multiple strategies may also be used, such as selecting species appropriate for the site, deep soil cultivation, and designing the space to maximize the distance between infrastructure and the tree. It is important to create the best match between the strategies and the site.

Developing proactive strategies for minimizing conflicts between trees and infrastructure can reduce repair costs and avoid tree loss. In the following tables, strategies, objectives, and practices are organized by whether the potential conflict exists around established trees (Table 2), around newly planted trees (Table 3), near sewer pipes (Table 4), or near structure foundations (Table 5).

Table 2. ESTABLISHED TREES: Reducing damage to infrastructure.

STRATEGY	OBJECTIVE	PRACTICE
A. Tree-Based Strategies		
Species selection	Select species compatible with the space available.	Select species based on knowledge of root development and trunk flare traits, size at maturity, and performance in similar sites. Avoid planting species in spaces that are not large enough to accommodate the root system and trunk flare at maturity.
Root pruning	Remove roots causing the damage while causing minimal damage to the tree.	Expose and prune only the roots that are causing damage. Make cuts as far from the trunk as possible. Minimize the number and size of roots to be cut. Some species do not respond favorably to root cutting. Avoid cutting roots on trees in poor condition, unstable trees, or old trees.

Table 2. (continued)

STRATEGY	OBJECTIVE	PRACTICE
Root shaving	Reduce a portion of a root that is lifting a sidewalk while minimizing tree damage.	Expose damaging roots and remove the upper portion of the root to increase the time before damage reoccurs.
Tree replacement	Eliminate the problem with the existing tree and install a less-damaging species to avoid future damage.	Either find an alternative location for tree planting or redesign the planting space.
Planting site abandonment	Eliminate the problem with the existing tree in the current site.	When the planting site is not adequate for tree development, the tree can be removed without replacement. An alternative, more favorable site nearby should be selected. This is the least preferred option.
B. Infrastructure-Based Strategies		
Increase size of planting space in sidewalk	Minimize the potential for root contact by enlarging the planting space.	Remove a section of existing sidewalk to increase distance from the trunk flare. Consider minimum widths for sidewalks and the accessibility requirements (e.g., ADA Standards in the United States).
Curving sidewalk	Increase distance between trees and sidewalk.	Redesign and replace section of existing linear sidewalk with sidewalk that bows or curves away from the trunk. Consider right-of-way issues.
Curb pop-outs	Increase distance between tree and curb.	Replace the existing section of linear curb with a new section that curves away from the trunk. Needs to be carefully engineered to avoid drainage issues, street-sweeping/snowplow conflicts, and interference with vehicles.
Narrower street	Increase space around trees (without infrastructure).	Redesign street to reduce width and create more infrastructure-free space for multiple trees. Several engineering considerations and requirements.
Bridging	Avoid the removal of roots causing sidewalk damage by bridging over them.	Replace existing sidewalk with new sidewalk elevated over roots that are to be preserved. Consider minimum slope and accessibility requirements (e.g., ADA Standards in the United States).
Reinforced slab	Reduce potential for concrete damage when roots contact sidewalk.	Concrete can be reinforced, typically with rebar, to reduce its potential for cracking. Reinforced slabs can still be lifted.
Thicker slab	Reduce potential for concrete damage when roots contact sidewalk.	In the United States, many sidewalks are 4 in (10 cm) thick. Increasing the thickness to be greater than 4 in may improve resistance to, but is not likely to prevent, cracking and lifting. Resistance to cracking is a function of the thickness of the base course as well as strength of the concrete. Consult a civil engineer when considering this approach.

STRATEGY	OBJECTIVE	PRACTICE
Modified expansion joints	Reduce potential for differential lifting of sidewalk slabs.	Insertion of steel pins or articulating joints between contiguous sidewalk slabs (at expansion joints) to avoid separation when one concrete slab is lifted by roots. Limited information regarding efficacy. Consult a civil engineer when considering this approach.
Rubber sidewalks	Avoid cracking and separation of slabs that are associated with concrete sidewalks.	Poured-in-place rubber or glued modules lift in unison (like a ribbon) to avoid slab separation associated with concrete can be used as an alternative to concrete. Can be colored to appear similar to concrete. More research information needed regarding limitations of use.
Ramps and wedges	Avoid tripping hazard associated with slabs that have lifted and separated.	Lifted edge of sidewalk slab is ground down to meet edge of adjacent slab (concrete shaving). Conversely, material (typically asphalt) may be applied to form miniramp or wedge between uneven edges of slabs. Both are temporary measures.
Pavers	Avoid cracking and slab lifting associated with concrete.	Used as an alternative to concrete. Pavers can be interlocking or not, and they are usually placed on a gravel and/or sand base, preferably 4 to 6 in (10 to 15 cm) deep or to local standards if greater than 6 in. Individual pavers or groups of pavers can be lifted by roots but can be replaced relatively easily after root shaving or removal or base modification.
Paver modules	Avoid cracking and slab lifting associated with concrete.	Paving modules that are larger than pavers and are interconnected. Modules lift in unison and can be removed and reinserted for root-pruning purposes. Information is needed regarding limitations to use.
Leveling pavement surface	Level adjacent pavement surfaces when one section was lifted by tree roots. Used to reduce tripping hazard and smooth surface.	Slab jacking and mud jacking are techniques that inject grout beneath a slab of concrete to lift it even with the adjacent slab.

C. Soil-Based Strategies

STRATEGY	OBJECTIVE	PRACTICE
Root barriers	Block and redirect roots away from infrastructure elements.	Materials (e.g., plastics and fabrics) installed between cut roots and infrastructure to block regenerated roots. Typically, placed in linear fashion along infrastructure element (e.g., sidewalk) and as close to the element as possible. Needs to be placed high enough to avoid root growth over the top edge. Roots that grow under the lower edge are no longer influenced by the barrier and can grow upward and under infrastructure elements.

Table 3. NEWLY PLANTED TREES: Reducing damage to infrastructure.

STRATEGY	OBJECTIVE	PRACTICE
A. Tree-Based Strategies		
Species selection	Match species size and growth characteristics with size of planting space.	Determine size of planting space and select appropriately sized species. Alternatively, identify size of tree desired for site and design planting space to accommodate mature size. Avoid species known to develop aggressive root systems.
B. Infrastructure-Based Strategies		
Design large planting spaces	Increase distance between tree and infrastructure.	Create and maintain as much distance between trees and infrastructure elements as possible. This strategy should be coupled with species selection. If large trees are desired, design planting spaces large enough to accommodate the tree when mature. For species that are large at maturity, it is best to plant new trees at least 6 ft (2 m) from any current or proposed infrastructure, or for the trees to be at least 4 ft away at mature size.
Monolithic sidewalks	Increase distance between tree and sidewalk.	Sidewalks installed contiguous with curbs and gutters and trees planted in space outside of sidewalk, typically in adjacent landscape. Compared with planting areas between sidewalks and curbs, the distance between trees and infrastructure is generally greater in monolithic sidewalk configurations.
Lowered sites	Increasing vertical distance between roots and infrastructure.	The planting site is designed so that the tree is planted below overlying infrastructure. In some cases, an air gap occurs between the soil surface and the lower surface of the infrastructure element. The potential for conflict is minimized because root development occurs below the element. Needs to be carefully engineered and can be expensive. Avoid planting trees too deep.
Tree islands	Increase planting space and soil volume for trees.	Plant trees in larger spaces as groups. Planting spaces can be mounded or not. Sidewalk alignment for this design is meandering rather than linear. Species selection and tree proximity to infrastructure need to be carefully considered.
Modified expansion joints	Reduce potential for differential lifting of sidewalk slabs.	Insertion of steel pins or articulating joints between contiguous sidewalk slabs at expansion joints to avoid separation when one concrete slab is lifted by roots. Limited information regarding efficacy.
Pervious concrete	Create soil conditions favorable for root development deeper below the sidewalk.	High-porosity concrete that allows water and gases to pass through and theoretically increases root development at depth. Little research evidence that soil aeration is improved or that a deeper root system develops. Concrete porosity may diminish over time if not maintained (e.g., by vacuuming).
Rubber sidewalks	Avoid cracking and separation of slabs that is associated with concrete sidewalks.	Used as an alternative to concrete. Rubber sidewalk modules or poured in place sections lift in unison (like a ribbon) to avoid slab separation associated with concrete. Can be colored to appear similar to concrete. More research information needed regarding limitations of use.

STRATEGY	OBJECTIVE	PRACTICE
Pavers	Avoid cracking and slab lifting associated with concrete.	Used as an alternative to concrete. Pavers can be interlocking or not and are usually placed on a gravel and/or sand base, preferably 4 to 6 in (10 to 15 cm) deep. Individual pavers or groups of pavers can be lifted by roots but can be replaced relatively easily.
Paver modules	Avoid lifting and cracking associated with concrete.	Paving modules that are larger than pavers and are interconnected. Modules lift in unison and can be removed and reinserted for root-pruning purposes. Information is needed regarding limitations to use.
Gravel layer under pavement	Create base layer that has load bearing capacity but is unfavorable for root development.	Rock or gravel ranging from 1 to 2.5 in (2.5 to 6.4 cm) reduces the potential for coarse root development while providing load bearing capacity.
C. Soil-Based Strategies		
Root barriers	Block and redirect roots away from infrastructure elements.	Materials (e.g., plastics and fabrics) installed between the tree **root ball** (or root system for bare-root stock) and infrastructure to block developing roots. Placed in linear fashion along infrastructure element (e.g., sidewalk) and as close to the element as possible. Needs to be placed high enough to avoid root growth over the top edge. Roots that grow under the lower edge are no longer influenced by the barrier and can grow upward and under infrastructure elements. Considerable research information regarding use and limitations.
Soil cells	Increase root distribution below infrastructure while providing support for the infrastructure.	Concrete or plastic structures that support infrastructure and provide rooting space below it. Soil for root development is evenly distributed throughout the volume which encourages uniform distribution of roots, particularly with depth. Needs to be carefully designed and engineered to meet needs of trees, particularly in arid or semiarid environments.
Structural soils	Increase root distribution below infrastructure while providing support for the infrastructure.	Replacement of a restrictive soil with manufactured media that includes a load-bearing component (rock or rigid frame) and that has sufficient depth and volume for root development. Soil for root development is evenly distributed throughout volume, which encourages even distribution of roots, particularly with depth. Needs to be carefully designed and engineered to meet needs of trees, particularly in arid or semiarid environments.
Soil cultivation	Improve soil conditions to increase root distribution with depth.	Roots restricted to the upper layer of soil due to a subsurface compacted layer (e.g., hardpan) or other restrictive condition are more likely to conflict with infrastructure elements than roots distributed deeper in the profile. Deep cultivation of restrictive soils improves the potential for deeper root development. Important considerations include soil compaction level needed to support infrastructure elements and the potential for soil settling over time.

Table 3. (continued)

STRATEGY	OBJECTIVE	PRACTICE
Root channels	Direct roots to grow away from infrastructure and toward favorable soil environments for root development.	Trenches or channels that emanate from the root ball, run under infrastructure elements, and end in larger soil volumes away from infrastructure. Channels filled with soil favorable for root development causes roots to be directed to the larger soil volume. This is a relatively new and unproven strategy that requires more information regarding root growth response, design requirements, and limitations of use.

Table 4. Reducing damage to sewers.

STRATEGY	OBJECTIVE	PRACTICE
A. Preventive Strategies		
Species selection	Avoid species known to have a high potential for root intrusion.	Consult local authorities or published references for species found to cause damage to sewer pipes. Avoid trees with relatively large crowns at maturity and fast-growing trees.
Planting distance from sewer pipes	Maintain maximum distance between new trees and sewer pipes.	Establish a minimum planting distance from existing pipes, such as 18 ft (6 m) or more for many species. The greater the distance between the tree and the pipeline, the lower the potential for root intrusion.
Placing new sewer lines	Maintain maximum distance between existing trees and new sewer pipes.	Identify existing trees and extent of root system. Design new sewer line to avoid the placement of pipes in the root zone of existing trees.
Block roots from entering joints	Minimize the potential that roots may intrude into joints.	Create fewer joints by using long pipe segments. Avoid using joint sealants that will weather or degrade over time. Ensure tight unions between pipe segments during installation. Consider using root barriers (horizontal and vertical) to block roots from developing near sewer pipes or place crushed rock around pipe and compact (refer to local building or engineering codes).
B. Remedial Strategies		
Root control treatment	Control roots that have intruded into sewer lines.	Mechanical removal of roots with specialized boring equipment. Consult local regulations concerning the use of herbicides. Both methods are temporary, as roots have the capacity to grow back into the sewer pipe.
Root cutting	Create zone around sewer lines that is free of roots.	Trenching between existing tree and sewer line to sever intruding roots. Compact soil as trench is refilled to minimize root regrowth into trench. Temporary measure if roots grow back into the trench. Consider installing root barriers in trench to block regrowth. Consider effects of root removal on tree stability and health.

Table 5. Reducing damage to foundations.

STRATEGY	OBJECTIVE	PRACTICE
Planting distance from foundation	Avoid root contact with the foundation.	The distance between damaged foundations and trees causing damage varies from 8 ft (2.5 m) for cypress (*Hesperocyparis* spp.) to 36 ft (11 m) for poplar (*Populus* spp.), with damage from most species occurring between 16 and 23 ft (5 and 7 m). In general, avoid planting large-stature trees within 25 ft (7.5 m) of foundations, especially in shrink-swell soils. Select small-stature trees and plant no closer than 16 ft (5 m).
Maximize depth of perimeter footings	Prevent roots from gaining access beneath the foundation.	The British National House Building Council guides that on a highly shrinkable soil, if a high-water-demand tree is located a distance equal to its height away from the foundation, the foundation should be 4.5 ft (1.5 m) deep. At half of that distance, a 7.5 ft (2.5 m) deep foundation is recommended. These distances may have to be modified for other climates.

Appendix 1
Contracting Root Management Treatments

When preparing contracts for inspecting or managing root growth, certain items should be included: the objective of the work; the treatment area or trees to be treated; methods, materials, and equipment to be used; and the time frame for completing the work.

Objective—The objective provides information on why the work is being performed. This may simply be to remove stem girdling roots or to reduce the potential of sidewalk lifting. More extensive information can be provided (if desired) to explain the reason for doing the work.

Treatment Area—The trees and area to be treated need to be clearly defined. For treatments that are applied to individual trees, it may be the address and tree location in the landscape. For root cuts, it may be a clearly defined line between two points. For root barriers, it may be a distance in two directions along the curb line, centered on the trunk of the new transplant.

Methods and Equipment—Because there are many ways to dig a trench or excavate a root collar, the contract should include the method that is to be used. It may specify a trenching machine, root cutter, supersonic air tool, or hand digging. The speed and cost of each of these methods and the skill level of the technician will vary greatly.

When installing a root barrier, the contract should specify material or product to be used or it may include only the barrier parameters, such as depth and length.

Time Frame—The contract should include the finished date or estimated work date.

Appendix 2

Root assessment is an option when conducting an Advanced (Level 3) tree risk assessment. Advanced assessments are conducted after or in conjunction with a Basic (Level 2) tree risk assessment.[4]

Generally, direct assessments of root health and distribution are not practical for established trees. Unlike the crown, the root system is not easily viewed. Soil covering root systems makes it very difficult or not feasible to assess root distribution (lateral, radial, depth), root loss, or root health (decay and disease).

Since the root system cannot be viewed, arborists need to consider both practices and factors (tree and site) that may contribute to root system failure. Table A2.1 lists several practices and factors to consider when assessing the potential for root failure. They apply to either or both of the two types of root failure: root plate lifting and root breakage. In some cases, both types can occur (lifting and breakage). Regardless of the type of failure, however, consideration of practices and factors that affect the potential for failure will help guide root system assessments and subsequent management practices.

---

4 See Smiley et al. 2017.

Root decay is often more prevalent on the underside of the root. This makes detecting root decay from above difficult. To verify the presence of decay, it may be possible to excavate around the root so that the bottom of the root can be probed or felt to determine if there is a loss of root tissue on the bottom side. If excavations of this magnitude are not practical, the root flare or structural roots can be sounded with a mallet or drilled to detect decay.

Roots or root flares can be struck with a plastic, plastic-covered, or nylon-covered sounding mallet to listen for variations in tone which can indicate dead or decaying roots. Typically, if there is less than 3 in (7.6 cm) of solid wood above the decayed area, tonal variation can be heard. However, sound can be dampened by surrounding soil, and tone varies with root diameter and among tree species. Therefore, this technique is not always successful.

Drilling roots or root flares with a small-diameter drill bit or resistance-recording drill may also help to determine the presence and amount of wood decay. The likelihood of root-related whole tree failure is based on many factors, including tree height, crown density, wind exposure, how much decay is present in individual roots, and the total number of main structural roots that are significantly decayed or cut. Roots are considered significantly decayed if the thickness of the sound wood on the top of the root is less than 0.15 times the tree diameter (DBH). When more than one-third of the main structural roots are significantly decayed or missing, the likelihood of failure is increased (Figure A2.1).

Fungal fruiting bodies associated with root decay tend to form on or very close to the colonized roots as well as buttresses and lower trunk. Mycorrhizal fungi and other nonpathogenic fungi tend to form fruiting bodies farther from the root or trunk, or in the mulch. Fruiting structures can be identified from photographs. Photographs submitted for expert identification should show both the top and bottom of the fruiting structure as well as a view of the structure on the tree part.

Wounds on roots can be caused by lawn mowers, string trimmers, animals, vehicles, foot traffic and excavation equipment. If wounds are limited to the top surface of a root, they tend to compartmentalize well, with minimal spread of decay and dysfunction within the root. However, more extensive decay may result from multiple wounds that coalesce and more often occur on tree species that are especially vulnerable to decay or that compartmentalize slowly.

Root cuts or root shaving which exposes the central regions (heartwood) of roots are more susceptible to wood decay fungi. If the decay is extensive, the likelihood of failure may be elevated.

Abnormal swelling at the base of the trunk may indicate that there is graft incompatibility, girdling, or internal damage/decay. **Sounding**, drilling, and **tomography** are methods and tools to help to determine the cause of the abnormal growth and the extent of internal damage.

Figure A2.1. Root decay is often more prevalent on the underside of the root (as depicted here by light grey zones). To verify the presence of decay, it may be possible to excavate around the root so that the bottom of the root can be probed or felt to determine if there is a loss of root tissue on the bottom side. Drilling to detect changes in wood density may also be used to determine the presence and amount of root decay.

Table A2.1. Practices and factors (tree and site) that tend to increase or decrease the potential for root system failure. These may occur alone or in combinations. For example, a tree with a dense crown in a windy area that has sustained root loss from a grade change can be considered to have a higher potential for failure than a tree with a dense crown in a windy area that has not sustained root loss.

Factor/Practice	Increased Potential for Root Failure	Reduced Potential for Root Failure
A. Management Practices		
Root pruning or cutting	Large percentage (greater than 33 percent) of root system cut/pruned/decayed	Small percentage (less than 25 percent) of root system cut/pruned/decayed
Roots cut (diameter)	Greater than 2 in (5 cm) diameter	Less than 2 in (5 cm) diameter
Roots cut (proximity to the trunk) on one side of the tree	Roots cut/pruned close (less than or equal to 3 x DBH) to trunk	Roots cut/pruned away (greater than 5 x DBH) from trunk
Root barriers (chemical and physical restrictions to lateral extension)	Barriers substantially restricting root distribution	Barriers that do not substantially restrict root distribution
B. Tree Characteristics		
1. Crown		
Tree height	Greater than 50 ft (15 m)	Less than 35 ft (10 m)
Density (branches & foliage)	Dense crown	Open crown
Live crown ratio (LCR)	Less than 33 percent	Greater than 50 percent
Crown balance	Unbalanced (e.g., one sided)	Balanced/centered
Lean	Significant lean, changing angle	No lean, stable position
2. Root System		
Decay	Extensive decay (greater than 33 percent of roots)	Decay not extensive (less than 25 percent of roots)
Disease	Extensive root loss	Little or no disease
Root distribution: depth	Shallow root system (less than 1 ft [0.3 m])	Deep root system (greater than 3 ft [1 m])
Root distribution: radial	Radial distribution is not uniform (e.g., one sided)	Uniform radial distribution (like spokes in a wheel)
Root architecture	Kinked, girdling, or circling roots	Relatively straight and well-branched roots

Factor/Practice	**Increased** Potential for Root Failure	**Reduced** Potential for Root Failure
C. Site		
1. Above Ground		
Wind exposure	High wind (e.g., coastal, mountaintop, building corners)	Little or no wind (e.g., protected by other trees or buildings)
Wind direction	Other than prevailing	Prevailing
Wind gusts	Frequent and strong	Little or no gusts
Changes in wind exposure	Increased wind exposure. Loss of surrounding trees or removal of adjacent structure	No change in wind exposure
2. Below Ground		
Soil moisture content	Wet or saturated soil, shallow water table.	Moist or dry soil
Soil depth	Shallow soils	Deep soils
Soil volume for root development	Small volume relative to tree size (e.g., large-stature tree in small soil volume)	Large volume relative to tree size (e.g., small-stature tree in large soil volume)
Terrain	Sloping terrain	Flat terrain
Erosion	Soil loss around the root system	No soil loss

Glossary

adventitious roots—root growth arising from roots, branches, or stems. They are true roots, but because they do not arise from a primary root axis, they are not one of the five basic types of roots. All roots arising from stem cuttings and occurring on palms are adventitious.

auxin—plant hormone or substance that promotes or regulates the growth and development of plants. Produced at sites where cells are dividing, primarily in the shoot tips. Auxin-like compounds may be synthetically produced.

base layer—the existing or added material to build a foundation upon.

buttress roots—lateral roots with buttressing that occur at the trunk base and help provide tree support.

calculated tree protection zone (calculated TPZ)—a TPZ that is calculated using the trunk diameter and a multiplication factor based on the species tolerance to construction and age of the tree. It is often plotted on a plan as a circle or other simple geometric shape.

DBH—acronym for tree diameter at breast height. Measured at 4.5 ft above ground in the United States, and 1.3 to 1.5 m in most other countries.

drip line—imaginary line defined by the branch spread of a single plant or group of plants.

fine roots—roots with a diameter of less than 2 mm that occur along lateral, sinker, and oblique roots.

fruiting body—reproductive structure of a fungus. The presence of certain species indicates decay in a tree.

girdling root—root that encircles all or part of the trunk of a tree or other roots and constricts the vascular tissue and inhibits secondary growth and the movement of water and photosynthates.

ground-penetrating radar (GPR)—a nondestructive technique that uses radar technology (electromagnetic waves) to image the subsurface.

hardpan–compacted soil layer nearly impervious to water, air, and roots.

heart roots–see *oblique roots*.

heartwood–wood that is inward from sapwood and is altered to provide chemical defense against decay-causing organisms while continues to provide structural strength to the trunk. Tree species may or may not have heartwood.

lateral roots–roots arising from the seedling tap root which grow horizontally from the base of the trunk and near the soil surface.

mycorrhizae–symbiotic association between certain fungi and plant roots.

nonselective root cutting–the indiscriminate severance of roots that often results in roots being broken or otherwise damaged.

oblique roots–roots that develop from the tap root and/or shallow lateral roots. Grow in an oblique or slanting angle.

preventive strategy–strategy employed to avoid future conflicts or damage, or to minimize the potential for conflicts.

remedial strategy–strategy employed after damage has occurred in an attempt to repair or minimize future damage.

root ball–soil containing all or a portion of the roots that are moved with a plant when it is planted or transplanted.

root collar–flared area at the tree trunk base where the roots and trunk come together (see *trunk flare*).

root collar excavation (RCX)–process of removing soil to expose and assess the root collar of a tree.

root flare (trunk flare)–transition zone from trunk to roots where the trunk expands into the buttress or structural roots.

root initiation zone (RIZ)–region at the base of a palm stem where lateral roots emerge.

root mat–dense network of roots. In palms, roots near the base of the stem.

root pruning–the cutting of tree roots to achieve a defined objective.

selective root pruning–the process of cleanly cutting roots to achieve a defined objective.

sinker roots–roots growing downward from lateral roots that provide anchorage and take up water and minerals. Especially useful during periods of drought.

sounding–process of striking a tree with a mallet or other appropriate tool and listening for tones that indicate dead bark, a layer of wood outside a cavity, or cracks in wood.

specified tree protection zone (specified TPZ)–a TPZ that is adjusted in size or shape to accommodate the existing infrastructure, planned construction, and specific aspects of the site, as well as the tree canopy conformation, visible root orientation, size, condition, maturity, and species response to construction impacts.

stem girdling root (SGR)–a root that grows tangentially across a stem causing vascular constriction (see *girdling root*).

structural roots–large, woody, tree roots that anchor and support the trunk and crown. They are characterized by secondary thickening and relatively large diameter.

sunburn–injury to the bark and cambium caused by a combination of tissue heating (sun exposure) and dehydration.

tap root–central, vertical root growing directly below the main stem or trunk that may or may not persist into plant maturity.

tomography–a picture of internal wood density generated by sending sound waves through a trunk or branch and measuring the time it takes to reach multiple sensors. Typically used to measure the extent of decay.

tree protection zone (TPZ)–area within which certain activities are prohibited or restricted to prevent or minimize potential injury to designated trees, especially during construction or development.

tree risk assessment–a systematic process used to identify, analyze, and evaluate tree risk.

trenching–linear or curved open excavation, often used to install utilities or structural footings.

trunk flare–see *root flare*.

water table–upper level of groundwater in the soil.

Selected References and Other Sources of Information

Benson A, Koeser A, Morgenroth J. 2019. Responses of mature roadside trees to root severance treatments. *Urban Forestry & Urban Greening.* 46:126448.

Benson A, Koeser A, Morgenroth J. 2019. A test of tree protection zones: responses of live oak (*Quercus virginiana Mill*) trees to root severance treatments. *Urban Forestry & Urban Greening.* 38:54–63.

Benson A, Lawson I, Clifford M, McBride S. 2021. Using robotics to detect footpath displacement caused by tree roots: a proof of concept. *Urban Forestry & Urban Greening.* 65:127312.

Biddle PG. 1998. *Tree Root Damage to Buildings.* Vol. 1. *Causes, Diagnosis and Remedy.* Wantage (UK): Willowmead Publishing Ltd. 376 p.

Costello LR, Jones KS. 2003. *Reducing Infrastructure Damage by Tree Roots: A Compendium of Strategies.* Cohasset (CA, USA): WCISA. 119 p.

Cutler DF, Richardson IBK. 1989. *Tree Roots and Buildings.* Harlow (Essex, UK): Longman Scientific & Technical. 71 p.

Fraedrich BR, Smiley ET. 2001. Assessing the failure potential of tree roots. In: Smiley ET, Coder KD. *Tree structure and mechanics conference proceedings: How trees stand up and fall down.* International Society of Arboriculture. p. 159–164

Hilbert DR, North E, Hauer R, Koeser A, Mclean D, Northrop R, Andreu M, Parbs S. 2020. Predicting trunk flare diameter to prevent tree damage to infrastructure. *Urban Forestry & Urban Greening.* 49:126645.

Hilbert DR, Koeser A, Moffis BL, Rowell JWG, McLean DC. 2020. How much space does my shade tree need? Planting space recommendations for medium and large trees in Florida cities. FL, USA: University of Florida. Report No. ENH1328/EP592.

Koeser AK, Hauer RJ, Hilbert DR, Northrop RJ, Thorn H, McLean DC, Salisbury AB. The tripping point–minimum planting widths for small-stature trees in dense urban developments. *Sustainability.* 14(6):3283.

Kourik R. 2015. *Understanding Roots.* Occidental, CA: Metamorphic Press. 225 p.

Kristoffersen PB, Bühler O. 2008. Case studies COST C-15, WGB: expanding root zones below sealed surfaces: structural soils. In: *Improving relations between technical infrastructure and vegetation: final scientific report. COST Action C15.* European Cooperation in Science and Technology.

Matheny NP, Clark JR. 1998. *Trees and Development: A Technical Guide to Preservation of Trees During Land Development.* Champaign (IL, USA): International Society of Arboriculture. 184 p.

McPherson EG. 2000. Expenditures associated with conflicts between street tree root growth and hardscape in California, United States. *Journal of Arboriculture.* 26:289–297.

Morgenroth J. 2008. A review of root barrier research. *Arboriculture & Urban Forestry.* 34(2):84–88.

Östberg J, Martinsson M, Stål Ö, Fransson A-M. 2012. Risk of root intrusion by tree and shrub species into sewer pipes in Swedish urban areas. *Urban Forestry & Urban Greening.* 11:65–71.

Randrup TB, McPherson EG, Costello LR. 2003. A review of tree root conflicts with sidewalks, curbs, and roads. *Urban Ecosystems.* 5:209–225.

Roberts J, Jackson N, Smith M. 2006. *Tree Roots in the Built Environment.* Vol. 8. *Research for Amenity Trees.* Norwich (UK): The Stationery Office. 288 p.

Scharenbroch BC, Smiley ET. 2021. *Soil Management for Urban Trees.* 2nd Ed. Best Management Practices. Atlanta (GA, USA): International Society of Arboriculture. 70 p.

Smiley ET. 2008. Comparison of methods to reduce sidewalk damage from tree roots. *Arboriculture & Urban Forestry.* 34(3):179–183.

Smiley ET, Matheny N, Lilly S. 2017. *Tree Risk Assessment*. 2nd Ed. Best Management Practices. Atlanta (GA, USA): International Society of Arboriculture. 86 p.

Smiley ET, Urban J, Fite K. 2019. Comparison of tree responses to different soil treatments under concrete pavement. *Arboriculture & Urban Forestry*. 45(6):303–314.

Smiley ET, Watson GW, Fraedrich BR, Booth DC. 1990. Evaluation of soil aeration equipment. *Journal of Arboriculture*. 16(5):118–123.

Smiley ET, Werner L, Lilly SJ, Brantley B. 2020. *Tree and Shrub Fertilization*. 4th Ed. Best Management Practices. Atlanta (GA, USA): International Society of Arboriculture. 57 p.

Smiley ET, Wilkinson L, Fraedrich BR. 2009. Root growth near vertical root barriers after seven years. *Arboriculture & Urban Forestry*. 35(1):23–26.

Urban J. 2008. *Up by Roots: Healthy Soils and Trees in the Built Environment*. International Society of Arboriculture. Champaign (IL, USA). 479 p.

Wong TW, Good JEG, Denne MP. 1988. Tree root damage to pavements and kerbs in the city of Manchester. *Arboricultural Journal*. 12(1):17–34.

About the Authors

Laurence R. Costello, PhD, is a horticultural and arboricultural consultant in San Francisco, California. He received his PhD in plant physiology from the University of California, Berkeley and MS in horticulture from the University of California, Davis. For 30 years, he conducted an education and applied research program in urban forestry and landscape horticulture in the San Francisco Bay Area for the University of California. He is a member of Western Chapter ISA and has served on the ISA Certified Arborist® Test Committee, BCMA Test Committee, and Science and Research Committee. He is an associate editor for *Arboriculture and Urban Forestry*.

Gary Watson, PhD, is lead scientist at The Morton Arboretum, working on root development of trees in urban landscapes. Dr. Watson has received the Award for Arboricultural Research, the Richard W. Harris Author's Citation Award, and Honorary Life Membership from ISA, and the Award of Merit from the Illinois Arborist Association. He is a past president of ISA, the Arboricultural Research and Education Academy, and the Illinois Arborist Association. He was the organizer and coeditor of the proceedings for the Landscape Below Ground and the Trees and Building Sites conferences.

E. Thomas Smiley, PhD, is a senior arboricultural researcher at the Bartlett Tree Research Laboratories (PNW). He serves on the ANSI 300 Standards for Tree Care Operations Committee. He has coauthored many of the ISA Best Management Practices, the 10th edition of the *Guide for Plant Appraisal*, and other publications. He received his PhD from Michigan State University, MS from Colorado State University, and BS from the University of Wisconsin–Madison.

Richard Hauer, PhD, is a professor of urban forestry at the University of Wisconsin–Stevens Point, teaching courses in urban forestry, nursery management, woody plants, dendrology, and introduction to forestry. He received the L.C. Chadwick Award for Arboricultural Research from ISA and the Excellence in Teaching Award from the University of Wisconsin System Board of Regents. He serves on the ANSI A300 Standards for Tree Care Operations Committee. He is also an associate editor of the journal *Urban Forestry & Urban Greening*.